About the Author

Farris Baker is a pastor and local businessman living in the Central Valley of California. His life of working in both the private sector and the public sector as well as for profit and non-profit experience has given him a broad view of society. He has supervised and managed people in both the non-profit, local government, and the business world giving him a broad look at society that many never see. Farris has a way of creating pictures in the mind to demonstrate common principals found in everyday life to make them easier to understand and apply to our lives in a practical since. As you digest this writing, you will see that practical issues for our lives are presented in a matter of fact way that is easy to understand and apply the benefits as well.

Introduction

The first thing that may come to mind about the title of this book may vary between readers depending on your background. Folks with knowledge of the Bible may instantly think of the Biblical character Jezebel and ponder what I may say about her from a strictly Biblical point of view and that is not what this book is about. Also it's not about that gal in the office that wears too much makeup either. Others may not know the Bible story of Jezebel and have no clue where I am going in this book or the human character that is applied to Jezebel. Others may reject the book just on the basis of my drawing from a story in the Bible and applying it to the modern work place. I think all readers even those of other religions or no beliefs at all will see the simple patterns that often are present in the work place that parallel in great detail the life of Jezebel in the Bible. This book's primary purpose is to explain patterns of behavior that cause serious problems in leadership in the market place as well as many other organizations and not to convert one to my specific religious belief system. So give the book a chance and I think you will be happy you did, you may even recognize yourself in some way!

Chapter One

Who Was Jezebel of the Bible?

In my introduction I say my primary goal is not to convert you or sway you to my way of thinking and of course the first chapter is about the Bible. The purpose of this first chapter being about the Bible is so the reader can come to the knowledge of the Bible story is to see how the original Jezebel behaved, what motivated her, and who did she influence with her behavior. So let's begin.

Jezebel is first mentioned because she has become the wife of a King of Israel, Ahab. There after her name is only mentioned nineteen other times in most translations of the Bible. Her life and character issues were so disdained that though an unsavory character of the Old Testament she finds her way to be mentioned in the New Testament as well.

1 Kings 16:31 And it came to pass, as if it had been a light thing for him to walk in the sins of Jeroboam the son of Nebat, that he took to wife Jezebel the daughter of Ethbaal king of the Zidonians, and went and served Baal, and worshipped him. **KJV**

In the passage above is where Jezebel comes onto the scene and we find out about her heritage and a few things about her husband. Jezebel's husband, who is not mentioned by name in this passage but eluded to, is King Ahab. Ahab was a very wicked man and adding to his wickedness he marries this woman Jezebel of a complete different culture and belief system. Ahab was a part of the nation of Israel and the life style and belief system of this people group was well established and exhorted to be continuous and consistent. The Zidonians in which Jezebel was a part of were a people with belief systems very different and contrary to the Hebrew life style.

Now as I progress through this story please trust me that there is an application to your work place or within your organization that I will clearly show you. There are many spiritual applications here as well which I will not go into detail on that is not the point of this book. If you are interested in further material on the spiritual implications I have others works that go in depth in that area.

In this first chapter I want to summarize Jezebels life and then through the remainder of the book we will see what makes her tick and where this pattern of her behavior is showing up in the work place or your organization.

References to Jezebel are found in the following five Old Testament Chapters I Kings chapters 16, 18, 19, and 21, as well as II Kings chapter 9 and one mention in the New Testament in Revelation 2:20. If you have a Bible get it out and read these chapters to familiarize yourself with the story. Another option to study the story is go online and listen to an audio version of the story. The Biblical account is brief and will not take you long however you obtain it. I will be making references as I move forward but a thorough review before hand is always good but not totally necessary.

Now that our king has married our bride Jezebel we find our royal couple leading as king and queen in Samaria. Samaria would be northern Israel of today. As a couple they are not honored as godly people but very much the opposite by history and the Bible.

The next detail we find out about Jezebel is that she does not like God's prophets and is in the process of having them all killed. Her actions against the prophets have them surviving on the run or in hiding to save their own lives. You will find references to this in I Kings chapter 18.

***I Kings 18:4** For it was so, when Jezebel cut off the prophets of the LORD, that Obadiah took an hundred prophets, and hid them by fifty in a cave, and fed them with bread and water.)*
KJV

In chapter 19 of I Kings Jezebel is told by Ahab about an encounter with the prophet Elijah in which he prevailed against Jezebel's own prophets. Elijah, God's prophet does amazing exploits which ends in the execution of most of Jezebel's prophets. Jezebel becomes infuriated by the actions of Elijah and vows that death will come to him as the other prophets.

Chapter 21 takes on a different path from the prophets fighting and we find King Ahab very sad and Jezebel is there to help him. King Ahab has found a plot of land that he wishes to have very much but the owner will not sell the land to him since it is his family farm passed on through the generations and very important to the owner, whose name is Naboth. When Jezebel hears of the situation she plots against the landowner and has false witnesses testify against him and has him executed for the things that he is being falsely accused of doing. With Naboth out of the way, in the end Ahab takes possession of the plot of land as an innocent man dies.

The last mention of Jezebel in the Old Testament is in II Kings chapter 9. In this chapter vows are made against Jezebel and she ultimately meets her end. Also through this chapter is a better known action of Jezebel in which she puts on her best makeup and hair-do and hangs out the window to be seen of all. This particular passage is what many think of when some one is referred to as a "Jezebel."

Her end is violent, thrown from a window to the street; her body eaten by dogs, and the truth of her evil doings were finally exposed and brought to an end.

Jezebel's last mention in the Bible is in the book of Revelation chapter 2 verse 20.

Revelation 2:20 *Notwithstanding I have a few things against thee, because thou sufferest that woman Jezebel, which calleth herself a prophetess, to teach and to seduce my servants to commit fornication, and to eat things sacrificed unto idols.* **KJV**

In the passage of Revelation an admonition against a New Testament church is being made. In this admonition they are told, paraphrasing it, you are behaving like Jezebel. Jezebel had set the standard for an evil way of life and she was so to say, the benchmark of wrong and evil, even in the New Testament. Nearly five hundred years after Jezebel's death, her influence and standard of evil was noted and used as an example to people of that day.

As I move forward we will look at her every move and I will show you how this pattern of behavior is still at work over 2500 years later.

Chapter Two
Bad roots, Bad tree, Bad Fruit

As I mentioned, the beginning of Jezebel we find that she is from a very different culture. In all of our lives we see so many examples in life that bad beginnings often bring about bad endings as well, Jezebel produces this kind of bad results.

***1 Kings 16:31** And it came to pass, as if it had been a light thing for him to walk in the sins of Jeroboam the son of Nebat, that he took to wife Jezebel the daughter of Ethbaal king of the Zidonians, and went and served Baal, and worshipped him.* **KJV**

Jezebel is from Zidon and she has married a Hebrew king, Ahab. We are talking about culture clash of major significance. This would be as extreme as an atheist marrying a devout religious person or far left liberal marrying a far right conservative. The Jews believed in one God and were to uphold a strict standard of life while the Zidonians were polytheistic and had a much more open culture. My point here isn't to promote the Jewish culture over the Zidonian culture but to show they are very different. Now even King Ahab was not adhering to his own culture and heritage so marrying this woman, Jezebel, went along with his pattern of failures and was quite easy for him to do.

Before I go further I want to be clear that the story of Jezebel is about a woman but both men and women can perform the behavior that I am exposing. Remember also that Ahab was a bad fellow in the story as well. Throughout this book I will be referring to types a "Jezebel" or an "Ahab" and though the character was male or female in our society today a man or woman could take on any of these roles and characteristics. In no way are these names and types exclusive to one sex.

This is the root of many problems in the work place or in your organization, culture clash. As we move through the life of Jezebel in detail and see the full manifestation of her behavior, this bad beginning will make much more sense and produce a bad ending.

This nation of Israel was to live by a particular standard, they themselves had drifted off course and now Jezebel was on the scene to take it even further off course and off course at a greater speed. Now you need to realize that each one of us sets a standard of some sort in our lives. These standards could be set by our belief systems or just by the standards our parents, schooling, or maybe military service that we have experienced. The people we work with or serve with in any organization have standards as well. The problem for us is when we find ourselves in an organization or work place and realize the people of influence and or in key leadership roles have a different culture of standards than as you do.

Ahab subjects his countrymen to another culture that was detrimental to the culture his people had come to expect. As king, Ahab was the one with the power to let this cycle of destruction begin or bring it to an end. The question may be asked why he did he let this change and destructive influence into in country. Those roots may be very clear as well. Marrying the daughter of a neighboring king more than likely brought great favor and protection from enemies as well as Jezebel may have been very beautiful. In our world today we call this by several names, "The Good Old Boy System" or may "You scratch my back and I will scratch yours."

Whether you are a leader or a subordinate employee or member of an organization we all have witnessed promotions and hiring practices that were paybacks, so to speak, to gain favor. We see relatives of people within an organization or of people of influenced hired or promoted before other qualified candidates not because of their qualifications but the influence of their relative or some one else. Ahab may have been operating this way looking for favor from a neighboring king. In any case King Ahab was looking out for number one, himself.

In life today this does happen just as well every day in business and other organizations. A person with different values or standards just slips in and is not really seen as a problem until the problems begin. In this case there may not be anything you can do to prevent this, especially if you are not in a position of influence yourself.

Once in the door Jezebel begins her work.

Chapter Three
Kill the Prophets!

We first need to define what a prophet does and how does that relate to all of us even in a non-religious environment.

1 Kings 18:4 *For it was so, when Jezebel cut off the prophets of the LORD, that Obadiah took an hundred prophets, and hid them by fifty in a cave, and fed them with bread and water.)* ***KJV***

A prophet is a person by Biblical definition that hears and proclaims the heart and mind of God. Prophets in essence are the mouth piece of God. Prophets told others what they were receiving from God and many of the things were predictive in nature and discerning of the times, both bad things and good things. With that said we can say that prophets are people releasing truth or maybe even common practice for the environment of your work place or organization.

An example of this could be some one that is a seasoned worker in a factory. They know the life and maintenance character of the equipment, maybe the vendors that service the factory. They also know the employees, their strengths and limits and where each of them is best suited for the factory. This seasoned worker knows how things work both good and bad because he has seen the history and lived and worked through it with previous successes and failures. We can say he has the truth about the factory and when allowed, can give valuable input as to the success of operations. This example can be found in most all organizations even to a point that a seasoned line worker may know as many or more details about the operation than an owner. If we look at our work place or an organization we belong to, we will find one or many such people that know the place and or operations very well. These people are invaluable to success and efficiency because they possess this true information or the truth of the organization and can help it prosper.

When Jezebel comes on the scene, she has a different culture than the proper culture and those that adhere to the correct way or the historical way are a problem to her. She is not worried about the correct way; she has chosen to do things a new way, the way of her culture.

I want to be clear that I am a proponent of modernization and I am not saying that Jezebel wants to modernize an organization. She is bringing something new but it is not all good, it is only good for her and those she likes. Obviously new people are brought into organizations to bring about changes that are positive and in no way would this apply to a Jezebel which brings about bad or different things of personal preference.

As these people that have the truth (prophets) see her selfish and irresponsible behavior they declare the truth. Jezebel is doing things that will hurt or cripple the organization because she is from a different culture and believes her ways are the best. Let's return back to the seasoned factory worker to be our prophet in this scenario. Jezebel the new foreman/manager says the machinery is running fine, she says let's cut back on maintenance to save some money and increase production with less down time. Her culture says look good by saving some money now with a lack of planning for the future. The seasoned factory worker (prophet) with the truth says, you can't do that because this machine will break down and it will shut down the entire operation for more time, unexpectedly, and at a greater overall expense. The seasoned employee (prophet) with the truth has now offended the Jezebel leader. At this point the Jezebel leader begins looking for opportunity to silence this seasoned worker with the truth, just as Jezebel of the Bible silenced Bible prophets with death.

In the Bible story, Jezebel rounds up and physically kills the prophets to silence them. Obviously we don't have rampant acts of murder in the work place but this type of person will go for character assassination or any other means to silence the out spoken critic of the new policies. The modern day Jezebel begins a campaign to discredit her opponent by looking for everything she can find to make them look bad. She goes about by changing work schedules, denying vacation time, or anything she can do to harm or discourage the person of truth and to harm their reputation in the organization. Her goal is to make anyone that opposes her plan for the business or organization to suffer and hopefully quit or create a situation so that they could be transferred or terminated.

Fear is generated as she begins persecuting those with the truth that have a culture that does not match her culture for the work place or organization. Now others that know the truth must go into hiding for fear of their own wellbeing. This hiding place for other prophets maybe just keeping quiet and not voicing their opinion. As the purveyors of truth are identified she takes them out one by one until she can operate totally unopposed. An organizational environment is established that is very intimidating to one group of people and full of favoritism to other certain people that agree and accommodate the new changes of culture.

I can share several personal experiences where just such things were done to my self to silence me. At one place I worked a new foreman was hired basically to be a hatchet man so to speak. This hiring was done to correct some issues but was done because current management had not corrected some issues themselves and this man turn out to be a poor choice to do the job. This man (Jezebel) would do the dirty work of management but was relatively out of touch with current operation standards of the business we were operating in at this time. This person gave dated and impractical dictates in the business that made little sense compared to modern operating standards. Myself, young and zealous for the truth and right practices began complaining and soon I found myself moved from the day shift to the night shift in retaliation. Eventually I looked for another job and left the place because of the poor work environment that was created. I was thoroughly character assassinated by this person for my opposition to his different culture or way of thinking that he operated under and was tolerated by the Ahab of the company.

In a sense we are just getting acquainted with Jezebel and already I am sure you are thinking about where she has shown up in your own life.

Chapter Four

Hide the Prophets

Now that we know why Jezebel wants to kill the prophets or those that oppose her workplace/organization culture, what is one to do if you are the person with the truth?

1 Kings 18:13 Was it not told my lord what I did when Jezebel slew the prophets of the LORD, how I hid an hundred men of the LORD'S prophets by fifty in a cave, and fed them with bread and water? **KJV**

Unfortunately hiding or laying low is the best policy at times. A fellow named Obadiah hid the prophets of God from the real Jezebel until she was out of the way, then they returned to normal life. The question is when will normal life return?

In our world today many organizations have advocacy groups as well as labor laws and such that protect people. As I described my plight of being transferred to a night shift in literal retaliation against me, I had a union representing me that could do nothing about the situation because there were enough loop holes for the Jezebel of my work place to retain this move. Jezebel may be evil but she is not necessarily dumb.

Being an advocate for what is right can mean death and if you are not willing to die for your cause you must be hid. Now by willing to die I do not mean physical death but death of the plans for the future you have made. A tremendous battle in the work place with a Jezebel type could put a blemish on your work history that could affect obtaining other employment in the future. Often we look at our organization and think of how we can bring positive changes, take care of our career, and obtain a higher position of leadership or job satisfaction. These long range plans have to die sometimes if Jezebel remains in your work place or organization for a lengthy period of time. No one knows how long the reign of Jezebel will last and any specific company or organization, so likewise, no one knows how long you will have to hide from her and her ways.

Hiding is not fun. If you read the passage at the beginning of this chapter, it says the prophets were hid in a cave under crowded conditions and fed bread and water. Hiding today within an organization that is being missed managed can be so frustrating especially when you know things could be done better. Hiding for a prophet may be just not saying things or getting transferred to an area where the miss-management is not in your face so much. This is where one must decide is it worth going through this and when is the possibility of all this hiding to come to an end so that normal organizational functions can resume with Jezebel having left the organization.

Hiding in the work place when you have the desire to excel and be a good employee is very tough to live through and endure. There are many that are completely happy with hiding out because they have no desire to be standard setters or to excel with their career. The Bible prophets could have been in the public setting, interacting with others and having a positive influence but they had to hide in crowded conditions, in darkness, with a meager food intake and none of the normal pleasures of life. Think about how depressing their life in the cave was to them. How long can one take this hiding and suppression and is there an escape to something better, maybe another organization where you can flourish. As I described one of my experiences, I knew as well as my fellow employees, that our Jezebel had a five year contract with management and it seemed as if the management were not about to admit they had made a mistake in this hire. I had my choice to shrink back in my existence or find other work. I chose other work but looking back I might should have hid out and kept my mouth shut for a while. This is a decision we all must make and live with the decision of our choice. My Jezebel did not make it his full five years but that was unknown at the time I departed from the organization. The organization did realize that they had created a problem and lost good employees because of this man during his time at the company.

Depending where you are in life, career development or devotion will determine whether you hide, run, make a stand, or allow Jezebel to kill you. If people in power don't have enough wisdom to see they have placed someone of the Jezebel's disposition in a position of power, do you really want to be with that organization? Is the current situation long or short term? Is there somewhere where it is better? If I leave do I lose all the foundation I created in this organization such as seniority, vacation time, retirement, and possibly many other things. These and other questions you have to ask yourself as you decide what to do.

Chapter Five
Friends of Jezebel

You may think everyone hates Jezebel but sad to say she has friends too.

1 Kings 18:19 Now therefore send, and gather to me all Israel unto mount Carmel, and the prophets of Baal four hundred and fifty, and the prophets of the groves four hundred, which eat at Jezebel's table. **KJV**

Now Jezebel had her own entourage of prophets. These are the people that promoted her culture and what she called truth. In the Bible these people were prophets of her culture that were traditionally considered demonic in nature to the worship of God by the Hebrews. The same goes for the modern Jezebel, she has rejected the truth of the organization and is bringing a new truth or her culture and she needs a support group to do so.

The Jezebel of the Bible brought these other prophets from her culture into the nation of Israel and the modern Jezebel will do the same. How many times does a new manager come on the scene and has a list of friends they want to bring on that have invaluable talent that they say we just cannot do without? We have all witnessed this many times in our company or organization. Employees are hired, new vendors, and new equipment all to support the new ways of this new and different culture. Now many times when positive changes happen to a dated organization the same things will happen to modernize and this is great and is not the same thing. The difference is that Jezebel's changes do not bring positive changes that help the over all organization but bring changes that primarily benefit her.

We must be progressive in how we operate and if new people come into an organization with fresh ideas and the ability to streamline and make an organization or business more efficient and or profitable that is great and that is not what I am talking about. I am talking about some one personalizing an organization to match who they are and fixed to the limits of their life and desires.

Do to fear and limitations of releasing truth, Jezebel also recruits new prophets from within, you may call these people brown-nosers that have little if any convictions in their lives. As people see her power and character assassination they yield to her way and join her team. Mostly these people are about self preservation and wish to use the situation for self promotion. Some people are just deceived by the power and influence not realizing the change is destructive. Jezebel is so power hungry that she gladly accepts anyone who will support her and will promote and favor these people as she is assassinating the character of those that oppose her. In nature we refer to two organisms that benefit each other as having a symbiotic relationship. One of the most popular symbiotic relationships is that of a saltwater clown fish and a poisonous sea anemone. The clown fish brings food into the anemone and is protected as well by the poisonous tentacles in which the clown fish is immune. At no point does a clown fish wish to become a sea anemone nor at any point does an anemone wish to become a clown fish. These two creatures, the fish and anemone just serve each other's needs. The same is true about those that yield to Jezebel; they have a symbiotic relationship in which both parties use the other party for personal gain only. Jezebel is out for what she can get from a person and often people will do things they don't wish to do for the protection that Jezebel offers to them. In most cases when separated they will talk of there disgust of each other.

It is difficult for a portrayer of truth to hide from Jezebel and say nothing but her own prophets have no problem serving her.

Chapter Six
An Uprising Against Jezebel

Elijah the prophet has an uprising against the ways of Jezebel and kills her prophets in the audience of King Ahab.

1 Kings 19:1 And Ahab told Jezebel all that Elijah had done, and withal how he had slain all the prophets with the sword. **KJV**

Jezebel of the Bible physically killed God's prophets and Elijah physically killed Jezebel's prophets. As described in chapter three Jezebel today does not physically kill but works on character assassination. In a sense Elijah does the same only for good and with just cause. Now Elijah represents the prophet bringing the truth to the workplace or organization. He gets an audience with the king and without Jezebel present; Elijah is able to present a clear case of the truth. Any one of us finding ourselves working with some one like Jezebel that is bringing down the organization, costing money, and demoralizing the people we want to expose them to the highest level of management we can to stop the destruction of the organization. Even better is to have the exposing meeting with Jezebel not present to cause a stir and or to stop the prophet from completing his mission. This is what Elijah did and the truth was obvious as he prevailed in killing all the false prophets. In today's world this would have been a closed door meeting with a person that had the truth and senior leaders with the person causing the problems not invited. In most cases today's Elijah better have some clout and reputation or he will never get this meeting. Separating a high level leader and demonstrating what is going wrong because of a Jezebel type person you would hope would vindicate your cause. This didn't work for Elijah, though he did have a big victory, and sometimes it does not work for us as well. Remember this management is who placed Jezebel in power and to remove her means they are admitting to making a mistake, most people are not that humble.

If leadership is truly seeking to have their operations work correctly, this may be the break through you need. They may see your evidence, the hypocrisy of those supporting Jezebel and call for change. One would hope truth would prevail.

Elijah, like many of us did not prevail but Jezebel was enraged at his actions and threatened his life.

1 Kings 19:1 And *Ahab told Jezebel all that Elijah had done, and withal how he had slain all the prophets with the sword. 2 Then Jezebel sent a messenger unto Elijah, saying, So let the gods do to me, and more also, if I make not thy life as the life of one of them by to morrow about this time.* **KJV**

Unfortunately someone has to make a stand and so to speak and put their head on the chopping block as Elijah did. The next thing he did was run for his life. Making a stand in the work place or your organization is not easy and takes courage and the results are not always the way you would like it to be. As I have said I made a stand in one company that I was employed with, and was punished by giving me an undesirable work schedule and jobs that eventually influenced me to seek other employment. Had management looked at my complaint in rational terms they may have made changes that would have retained me in their employment. Over time after I had departed, other situations vindicated me and the Jezebel of that work place was removed, too late for me but the company may have been influenced by my actions.

31

Chapter Seven

How Jezebel Keeps Her Position

If Jezebel is so awful how does she keep her position? Jezebel may be serving a greater purpose that is desired by leaders, than the destruction she brings in other areas. Remember Jezebel in the Biblical story is the king's wife, not just any woman. She is woman that the king has made a commitment of marriage. This too is the entanglement that takes place in an organization. A contract or maybe an election takes place and a commitment for a period of time is expected to be kept with Jezebel. All intents and purposes from the beginning is that things are going to work out well and when they don't, there is the contract for a period of time.

1 Kings 21:5 But *Jezebel his wife came to him, and said unto him, Why is thy spirit so sad, that thou eatest no bread?* **KJV**

Who can make the king happy? King Ahab was sad because he was denied the purchase of a piece of land. This is how Jezebel retains her position and influence by bringing happiness in an area that really upsets leadership. In the Biblical story Jezebel defamed the character of the land owner and had him killed so that Ahab could take possession of the land. In a sense, Jezebel becomes the hatchet man or is willing to take on the dirtiest job to win favor and power with leadership. Because higher up leadership does not like doing the dirty work they especially like when someone (Jezebel) steps up to do the dirty work for them.

In the Biblical story everything about her actions to obtain the land and the desire of the king were immoral. The man that was killed did nothing wrong and was falsely accused and murdered without cause. False witnesses were recruited to defame his character and convict him of crimes he did not commit. In Jezebel's attack against this man, she says many things and does many things that sound very righteous, but in reality her actions were hideous and evil. Remember people are afraid of Jezebel so they will do as she asks because they do not wish to become her victims so she has no trouble finding help.

There are two possibilities for Jezebel to do the dirty jobs for leadership. The first is as in this Biblical account where an innocent man is destroyed for personal gain and the second is by leadership abandoning their responsibility.

You hear this term in politics, "Plausible Deniability." We see this in politics where the CIA employed a questionable practice outside of the knowledge of the President so that something could be done that was not a good thing for the President to order to be done. This action would be called rogue behavior when in truth the President may have been behind it all the time. So it is plausible that he can deny knowledge of whatever the CIA did own their own. Jezebel often provides "plausible deniability" to the Ahab's of their organization to gain favor.

In the first example leadership is corrupt and has personal goals that they use a Jezebel type person to obtain. In my personal example as soon as I was assassinated and left my employment, the son of the Jezebel person was hired to fill my place. With only a limited budget for positions and the desire to bring a family member into the organization a campaign to terminate another employee through character assassination or another means will take place. Someone becomes the target of elimination and as they are pushed out of the way the Jezebels will do as they please. Leadership are so grateful when someone does this for them that the leadership will overlook the other bad things that the Jezebel type person is doing that may be causing harm.

In the other case of leadership abandoning their responsibility, leadership may have just cause for disciplining someone or changing something but they are weak and do not like facing those kind of issues that may cause opposition or hard feelings. It could be that an employee needs to be fired or disciplined and the Jezebel person says I will do it. A great load is taken from leadership by this Jezebel person who is happy to be the hatchet man and do any dirty work thrown their way. Jezebel is not about making friends, she has a great lust for power, so offending people does not bother her if it gains her power. Termination or other actions of discipline on occasion need to be done but it needs to be done by the right person. Weak leaders that give the dirty jobs away end up giving excessive power to people that it does not belong too. A perversion of leadership structure begins to take place as power is yielded to the Jezebel. Leadership may become overly grateful and the

Jezebel person may use this favor to manipulate the leadership in other ways in the future. This particular relationship could be looked at as a symbiotic relationship as well, two separate ways of thinking and doing but serving each other in a way for personal gain and comfort.

Jezebel is looking for power and will do what she can to obtain it.

Chapter Eight
The Demise of Jezebel

The demise of Jezebel is imminent in time. The kind of self serving behavior meets an end in time. Whether a person of this nature shows up in organization or in the work place they must go or the organization or work place eventually will suffer and possibly collapse due to their behavior.

***1 Kings 21:23 And** of Jezebel also spake the LORD, saying, The dogs shall eat Jezebel by the wall of Jezreel.* **KJV**

God's prophet spoke of the destruction of Jezebel and it happened just like he said it would happen. The end that Jezebel wanted for those that opposed her came back her way. In the Biblical story the entire kingdom was turned upside down and truth and God's prophets came out of hiding and starting bringing things back into order. All the unjust acts had an accumulative effect as we commonly say "what goes around comes around," that is exactly what happened with Jezebel.

The demise of a Jezebel type person takes generally more than one person willing to put their reputation on the line for the truth. By the time someone steps up to take action many cases of character assassination and other acts of injustice have taken place. Some people have went into hiding while others have taken Jezebel's side and where is the current stance of higher up leadership, has to be asked before confronting this person.

In the Biblical account there are two prominent people that make a stand to bring Jezebel down. There is a man named Jehu and the successor to Elijah, Elisha also a prophet. You might say Elisha proclaims the truth and Jehu enforces truth. During the Biblical account the culture is literally turned upside down to bring it back into order. When faced with Jezebel today are we willing to put our selves at such great risk to restore things to order?

2 Kings 9:30 And *when Jehu was come to Jezreel, Jezebel heard of it; and she painted her face, and tired her head, and looked out at a window.* **KJV**

The most popular knowledge of Jezebel is her last day with heavy makeup on her face and her hair fancied up for all to see. This is the image most think of when Jezebel is mentioned. What this is saying is that she was making one last effort to be seen and noticed to maybe stop the ultimate demise of her life and ways. She went down kicking and screaming so to speak and this is the issue when really facing this Jezebel type behavior, she is a major "drama queen." The biggest threats and accusations will come up in the heat of the last battle. Jehu had no fear of these because he had truth on his side. Much of facing something like this is keeping ourselves pure in our work habits and personal behavior so that we can confront things without having the fear of our own demons being revealed. People with less than a perfect record are fearful that their personal skeletons in their closets will be revealed. In times like this when the Jezebel person sees that he or she is about to face their demise is when Jezebel lashes out towards everyone in a last effort to survive and save her position and power. This could mean accusations of sexual harassment, labor law violations, discrimination, environmental issues, and maybe even other laws or policies being broken. If there is any validity to any of these charges Jezebel may be able to hold his or her power for a longer period of time showing that they are no worse than her accuser.

In the end the Bible Jezebel was tossed out the window by her personal servants and met her death as she hit the ground. This is the case in life today. There are many being hurt by people like this that are being silent and just waiting for and opportunity to see justice take place. You may be surprised at who will come forward when Jezebel is properly confronted and they feel safe to speak. Even appearing loyal servants that are very close to Jezebel may turn when the opportunity arises. When a righteous voice rose up, Jehu, the personal servants jumped up to help immediately and Jezebel was stopped right there on location.

Chapter Nine
Who Are You In This Story?

Sad to say that in the way life plays out and depending how old you are, you possibly could have been anyone of the characters in the story, just as me. In the next few chapters I will discuss each of the characters that you may see where you are in your workplace or organization.

I would hope that this book would be used as a pattern for bringing right behavior among people as well as teach a pattern for recognizing destructive behavior and selfishness. I would encourage all to be on the side of right thinking and consideration for all.

Please be objective as you read the next chapters, judge yourself. No one wishes to be found guilty of something bad but if you have fell into the trap and began taking on the character of Jezebel or Ahab, admit it and do your best to make amends for your wrongs and change your ways.

I worked for one foreperson in the past that made this statement, "Our employer takes good people and makes them into bad people." This foreperson was right to a degree but wrong in the fact. Because of bad conditions and injustices the good people choose to give up and join the injustices instead of retaining their integrity and rising above things. Hang in there and do what is right!

Chapter Ten

Living the Life of Jezebel - Its Good For a While

I would hope no one would intentionally take on this role but some do; there are actually other things in our society that are worse. Please be objective as you judge yourself. Look close to see if you have some of these patterns in your life then look at others.

Jezebel From Another Culture

One of the first things to know about being a Jezebel is that he or she is from another culture. By another culture I mean a different set of moral or traditional values and is an extremely self-serving person. I do not mean a different ethic or religious culture I am strictly referring to the culture of a work place or an organization. If the organization was of a particular ethic culture or religion then this could fit but I am not referring to that in this book specifically.

When a person comes to a new organization and they feel totally out of place they may have a different organizational culture. One would have two choices not being of the same culture, the first adapt to the current culture and the second, change and influence the culture when opportunity arises or opportunity is made. All of us feel more comfortable and accepted when we are surrounded by those that agree with us.

Adapting to a new culture excludes you being a Jezebel. You are humbling yourself coming to a new culture and blending to the new surroundings in a peaceable and respectable manner.

Jezebel Wants Change

If you are desiring change want is your motive? Why did you come to this place or why were you brought to the organization? If an organization has drifted off course or is out of date and upper management has brought you in to bring the organization into a better place you are not being selfish as Jezebel but being a positive influence to bring about positive changes. On the other hand if someone has come on board and simply wants the organization to please themselves for their own personal reasons, one may call this person a Jezebel. Keep this in proper perspective, you could be personally pleased bringing about positive changes but we are looking at the greater good of morality and of the benefit of the organization. Again this isn't saying all change is bad, but how the change is brought about is the issue many times with Jezebel.

Jezebel Begins To Release Propaganda

As Jezebel begins to rise to power and influence she or he begins spreading propaganda to support her opinion and purpose for change. Propaganda is necessary because she does not have real truth for the organization. At first subtle comments are made and then as followers are recruited, bolder statements come forth that increase in setting the tone she desires. As an example of changing vendors that I mentioned in chapter five, Jezebel will be watching for mistakes of the current vendor and enlarge the problems and tell those that will listen as often as possible to build her data and case against the current vendor. As people begin to listen the solution will be presented which will be doing things his or her way, remove the current vendor and hire her friend that she claims is far superior. Jezebel will use this tactic in any situation she can to sway opinions and policies to gain her desired outcome.

You Are Being Marked

As Jezebel is doing his or her manipulation you are being categorized as being for or against the changes that are being proposed. If you have sided with Jezebel you will be promoted and if you have issues with the new thinking you will be talked about in a negative light. The purpose of this action is to build a team for change. Any team needs to be unified to be affective and even the Jezebel team. Jezebel will busy looking for and showing favoritism to those that agree and submit to his or her ideas and changes. Even being neutral is not good in most cases with Jezebel. She wants full support and neutrality is not a vote for her ways.

Unawares during this time that Jezebel is preaching change she is being heard by management. Wise and insightful managers should see through her actions but at this point Ahab type leaders are being attracted to her.

If upper management has hired this person for a leadership role, the Jezebel person will be carefully presenting those that oppose him or her in a very negative way to upper management to further buffer the Jezebel position. The more you oppose Jezebel's change the more you will be marked as a dissenter and a problem to the organization. Jezebel will be proclaiming that you should be eliminated or punished in some way for your opposition. If you support Jezebel, life will get easier for you and you may be promoted or your work burdens made easier. You can see how self-serving people thrive in this environment because public opinion is more important than facts or job performance.

Jezebel Is Feared

Whether you agree or submit to Jezebel there is a real fear that begins to develop in many parts of an organization as Jezebel gains power. There is a fear of retribution for opposition and there is a fear of collapse of the organization because of all the illogical self-serving behavior done by Jezebel and her surrogates. People subordinate to Jezebel are in fear that they must submit or pay the price. People above Jezebel may have fear as well wondering if all these changes are going to work their way out properly. The organization is in flux at this point, no one knows for sure where things are going if Jezebel has had her way for any period of time. If management has the Ahab behavior they are most likely oblivious to what is happening because Jezebel is doing things they do not wish to do and that makes them very happy. If management has allowed Jezebel to grow in power or hired a Jezebel by mistake they are generally feeling some fear right now as well. Upper management is saying to themselves, what kind of monster have we created and how are we going to save face and get rid of this person?

Punishment And Elimination Of Your Enemies
After the marking of enemies, Jezebel begins punishment and elimination. Depending on the organization or workplace and the actual position of Jezebel will depend on how Jezebel carries out this part of his or her behavior. If Jezebel is in a position to terminate your role in an organization that is her first choice. Some punishment and persecution can help you become riper for termination. Jezebel may take some of your work away, transfer you, or change your work schedule to upset you and punish you. As his or her opposition feel the attack against them they too will instinctively lash out at Jezebel. At this point Jezebel has one more thing to use against those that oppose her, insubordination. All of Jezebel's actions are carefully planned to achieve all of his or her

personal goals. Jezebel is happy you are angry because maybe you will leave or make a mistake that you can be further discredited to leadership and become an example to others of what happens to dissenters. All this punishment and elimination furthers the cause and generates the fear that gives Jezebel power. Those that were neutral in their position are now thinking about joining ranks with Jezebel, at least in word if not in deed.

Selfishness Eventually Brings Destruction
All the power that Jezebel has gained has been subversive in nature and not because of true qualifications and this can only last so long. Good employees have been lost and cowardly "yes-men" have replaced them, this is not the recipe for success. A business or organization needs good highly qualified people to survive and lead the organization on into the future. The selfish power hungry behavior of Jezebel has eliminated many of these people and the overall quality of the work force has suffered as well. Jezebel will say things are going great but the truth will begin to appear in the numbers and hard facts in the days and weeks ahead. Even upper management will begin to take a deeper

look at the behavior Jezebel as their finances begin to be challenged. Depending on the organization this could take a few months or a couple annual reports to really show up. At the first signs of failure Jezebel will deny and blame his or her critics for the problems. Once the critics are gone, there is no one left to blame but Jezebel.

Jezebel has become so manipulative that real life is less than real to them at this point. Jezebel has used fear and intimidation so much that self motivation and truth are almost illogical within the organization. When faced with real issues and a bottom line, the lack of qualifications and the lies becomes so evident, upper leadership will say that Jezebel must go.

In supporting his or her position and with the lack of integrity of Jezebel more than likely has policies and laws that have been broken right along with the ethical issues than have been present. Jezebel is doomed for destruction. Suddenly with no one else to blame, the truth that was being suppressed by her is now coming out to bring her down.

Chapter Eleven
Ahab, Master At Passing The Buck

To understand Ahab and to identify where he went wrong we have to first look at a couple things that are very obvious about the life of Ahab or an Ahab type person. First as we talk about Jezebel being of a different culture, Ahab is the one that brought Jezebel into this culture. Ahab is the one who went to a foreign land and married this woman Jezebel of a different culture. Obvious we in the business world may be in a place that your culture may need to change such as modernized or streamlined. Many times someone is brought into an organization without with a lack of wisdom (On Ahab's part) or poor interviewing skills or process and that person of a different culture arrives. Because of Ahab's nature, Ahab does not like to be the bad guy. Ahab's do not like to give bad news to others or deliver punishment. They like to put someone else up to do their dirty work. Whether they planned to bring a Jezebel type person into the organization or not when a Jezebel type person shows up the Ahab will take advantage of the Jezebel and use them to do their dirty work.

In a sense what you may say about an Ahab type person is that they are not really doing their job. Responsibilities that belong to them are passed off to a Jezebel person that will do the dirty works to gain favor for themselves. This becomes a symbiotic relationship. Like the clown fish that lives in the sea anemone and they help each other, Ahab and Jezebel help each other. The clown fish is immune to the poison of the anemone so it can hide where others would die. As the clown fish brings food to its safe poison abode, it feeds the anemone as it feed itself. Ahab wants all the dirty jobs done and Jezebel does these jobs for him. Jezebel's one strength is that she is willing to obtain that power by doing dirty jobs for Ahab.

To find an Ahab in an organization you will find a leader that can not handle being the bearer of bad news, firing people, telling people to do their job, or anything else where they may get negative feedback. An Ahab will be nervous and fret for days, putting off doing what is his job because he hates doing it so much. For instance if an individual is not doing their job and others are complaining and he knows he must do something, he is literally getting an ulcer thinking about telling this person to do their job. He procrastinates so long that the situation gets worse and worse and worse. He is waiting for Jezebel to come along, the person wanting power, to say "Would you like me to do that for you?" And when Jezebel will help, he says "Yes." He abandons his responsibility and gives power to Jezebel because he or she did his difficult tasks for him. To be loosed of this burden on his life, he is willing to give up control and at times common sense. This relationship grows and grows and Ahab begins to ignore all the bad attributes that Jezebel has and he rewards him or her instead. He gives great favor to Jezebel because Jezebel does the things that he hates to do.

So if you are in a position of leadership and you are not doing your job, you look for others to do the things that you dislike doing, you possibly are becoming an Ahab. Depending on your organization there are different solutions for this problem but the most basic is, one must do their job and take the good with bad. If handling certain aspects of your job that you feel that you are not cut out for performing, you are being dishonest with those that are relying on you to uphold the duties of your position. The only solution is to step down from the position or seek training to do those things that you dislike. You must stop passing the buck! Not being a true Hebrew King cost Ahab and his following generations to lose what belonged to them. Continuing to be a Ahab type leader will eventually take you out as well.

Chapter Twelve
Obadiah, Good Man in a Bad Place

The first thing many of us would think is that a corrupt organization or at least an organization that is not on a good course would be made up with individuals that have poor/corrupt work ethic from top to bottom. This is not true, there are always a few Obadiah's left in the organization. If you remember Obadiah, he hid the good prophets and cared for them but he also worked for Ahab who was party to killing some of the same prophets. Isn't this a contradiction? Of course it is but many are faced with difficult decisions many times. We have a vested interest in an organization and because it has shifted its focus, standards, and or efficiency we are not quick to walk away so we become an Obadiah.

You are an Obadiah if you continue to do your job, hold to policies and principles in spite of the degradation of the organization. You are motivated by the hope that someday things will turn around.

If we look back at chapter three you will remember this passage of the Bible where Obadiah is mentioned.

1 Kings 18:3 *And Ahab called Obadiah, which was the governor of his house. (Now Obadiah feared the LORD greatly: 4 For it was so, when Jezebel cut off the prophets of the LORD, that Obadiah took an hundred prophets, and hid them by fifty in a cave, and fed them with bread and water.) 5 And Ahab said unto Obadiah, Go into the land, unto all fountains of water, and unto all brooks: peradventure we may find grass to save the horses and mules alive, that we lose not all the beasts.* ***KJV***

Obadiah is the kind of person that secretly tries to maintain the things the way they were before a Jezebel came on the scene. Jezebel is destroying the good because they oppose her ways and Obadiah is covertly hiding the good for a day when things come around back to the good. Obadiah, a prophet himself, had a role very different than Elijah. He secretly opposed what was happening and set up himself for healing the organization in the future. Elijah on the other hand was a radical out in the open proponent for immediate change.

A person being the Obadiah of an organization is trusted by both sides. If you look at the passages from the Bible you will see that Obadiah had a position in this wayward organization of some power and influence and he was called upon in a time of need by Ahab, and he still covertly hid the true prophets. One might say that Obadiah was two faced and played all sides, while that may seem true and does happen, Obadiah was out for the best for the organization and maintained peaceful relations with all parties. This is not an easy role to live out.

Being in the position of Obadiah may appear that you are person of compromise and if your actions become exposed to either side of the issues and you may appear as for the other side. If Ahab or Jezebel had found out that Obadiah had hid the one hundred prophets and was caring for them, he may have signed his own death sentence. Likewise others opposed to Jezebel and Ahab see that Obadiah has a position of power in the organization might assume he is totally sold out for the side of Jezebel. Getting along with all sounds good but is a very dangerous and easily misunderstood place to be.

Chapter Thirteen
Elijah, A Thankless Advocate

Elijah is the likely central figure for the good guys of this story but again it is not an easy position to be in. In the work place we have all kinds of whistle blower protection that gives protection to Elijah types but in many organizations of all kinds, the Elijah's stand alone for their cause.

Two great things that you will do if an Elijah is your position; 1.) Declare the consequences of the change that has come to the organization and 2.) Declare the wrongs that have been committed. Ahab and Jezebel both will want to silence and discredit you for speaking up. As an example, if an organization had adopted a unsafe work practice and Elijah would say this work practice is unsafe and describe in detail why it is unsafe and then declare that the organization may have serious injuries, deaths, and legal action brought against it if this problem is not addressed.

As Elijah in the Bible literally ran for his life this sometimes happens to modern day Elijah's as well. Depending on whether you are with a for profit corporation, government, or a non-profit organization the consequences and available whistle blower protection may vary. Many times Elijah's retain their existence but are shunned by most and live out a very sad existence if things do not change or they adapt to the ways of Jezebel.

If you are contemplating to be an Elijah you must really think about the consequences that you may suffer for this right cause. Ask yourself the questions; can real change be made here? Would it be better if I moved on? How will this effect me personally and my family? How deeply committed are your Jezebel and Ahab figures to their goals? Are Ahab and Jezebel near retirement years? Is there an advocacy program or agency that could better deal with the situation?

At one point Elijah became and out right childish in his behavior. He cried out to God and said he was the only good person left. This is the feeling many times of being an Elijah, "I am the only one willing to make a stand for what is right." God straightened out and Elijah and reminded Elijah that there are many more that want correct behavior as well. You are not alone!

Chapter Fourteen
Jehu, The Hired Gun

Jehu really means new management. Jehu comes and finds all the mess and wrong doing of both Jezebel and Ahab and radically brings things back into order. I used the word radically to signify how great of changes are coming. Depending on how far off course the organization moved, the more radical the changes are needed to correct the course. A Jehu type may not even be possible if the organization is a sole proprietorship and the proprietor is living like an Ahab.

So if you have just taken leadership of an organization that was overwhelmed with problems you may have found yourself as Jehu or the next Ahab if you do not fix the problems. Who ever hired, assigned, appointed, or hired the new person to this position of leadership may not have disclosed everything that was going on in the organization. When searching for a leader to replace an Ahab type and take care of a Jezebel type, those with the hiring or appointment power are looking for a strong Jehu type. The problem is that possibly these same people appointed or at least allowed Ahab and Jezebel to have power previously, so their record in successful appointments is not too great. Therefore in the appointment of a person they are hoping to be a Jehu, they may have ended up with another Ahab or possibly a Jehu or some one who fits somewhere in between. Jehu represents radical correction of wrong and most likely is not going to be a long term leader. A long term leader most likely has accepted the leadership in an organization that is running smoothly and doesn't need radical changes and comes in and takes control and develops the organization to its potential with out war so to speak. Beginning your career as Jehu, with war, does not usually speak of long term service but one of coming in, fixing things, and then moving on to the next one. A Jehu is a warrior leader and may not fit once the war is over.

Even some good people who are fooled by Ahab and Jezebel, so when Jehu comes to an organization there are some that should initially be with Jehu's position of correction but may not be until they see the light. Jehu is not the kind of person to win the hearts of his people but is there to correct action and rid the place of Jezebel and Ahab and their traits upon the organization. As Jehu lives out who he is, he may be offending good people that were fooled by the behavior of Ahab and Jezebel thus not gaining these good people as allies but as enemies for a season. So when one finds themselves in this position as a Jehu, it is imperative to educate people as to why you are taking such action. In today's society with so many rules and laws that protect a person's past, a Jehu must be careful that he keeps a balance for being truthful about wrong past practices and not putting himself in the position of slandering and defaming the character of Ahab and Jezebel that proceeded his administration. A full blown Jehu is much better at wielding the sword than tickling people's ears, so to speak. Diplomacy that is needed may be difficult for Jehu as he wields his sword of correction.

To sum up Jehu, this is a person with a passion to get things straighten out with correct behavior more important than winning the hearts and support of all.

Chapter Fifteen
The Middleman, An Open Door for Jezebel

A Jezebel type is always looking for a way to get a foot hold on power in any organization and in this chapter I will describe a very common way this begins. This beginning is being a middleman. If you remember that Jezebel likes to do more difficult things for her Ahab to win his favor towards her. Being a middleman for various task is the first step many times for Jezebel to gain entry to this power.

Many managers or leaders of an organization get overwhelmed with various duties and there are always some tasks that they dread taking care of or are just not a satisfying to complete as other tasks. When one of these tasks is in front of a leader they may make a comment about their dread over completing a task they don't like. Jezebel is all ears for an opportunity like this complaint and is more than likely to hear about it. Remember Jezebel is looking for power and she has this façade that she puts on to get close to leadership just so she will be near when a complaint is said. Covertly she has been wooing the leadership and has been working on being in the right place at the right time to grab favor and power. So when

Jezebel hears this complaint or dread of a task she is ready to say that she is willing to help and offers her help even with pressure. Another task Jezebel is not beyond taking is one of having an intimate relation with her superior also to gain power and favor.

What is the dreaded task and how close is Jezebel already? First remember these dreaded task are the job of the leader, he or she is not doing their job if they give away these tasks to Jezebel. There are so many scenarios of organizations so it is impossible to give a complete list of task so I will give a few that many of us may be accustom with. The tasks could be writing reports, reviewing correspondence, entering data, answering or returning phone calls, attending low priority meetings, ordering supplies, and maybe scheduling appointments. As I said organizations very greatly so all of these may fit some places and none may fit other places, the key is that the leader is giving up his or her duty where their direct input is needed and they are trusting someone else will have the same input and task performance as they would have.

I am going to use returning phone calls as a further example. If our manager in this example is overwhelmed with voice mails and is frustrated with this task then he begins openly complaining about the messages and those that leave the messages. Jezebel has already been positioning herself and is most likely not noticed at this point and hears his complaints. She steps up and offers her services to help out. Jezebel is not just any employee; she is close enough that the manager feels comfortable complaining in her presence and possibly close enough to be trusted with reviewing and answering voice mails. Whether Jezebel gets this task or not she will be looking for more tasks as well to secure her search for power.

Assignment Accepted

Once Jezebel has received a task that is not hers she gets to work. She wishes to speedily and effectively finish this task to please and impress her leader. It is not a bad thing to help your boss out and do a good job; it becomes a problem when your motive is to seize power, power that does not belong to you. Jezebel will want this task to be a success so it will lead to more tasks and more power and more influence. As Jezebel works on these task her influence begins to grow and she filters and colors her work and the task begin to shift in character from the leader's character to her character. The first few assignments Jezebel will accurately represent her leader. As confidence in her ability and the peace of the task being lifted of the leader grows, Jezebel begins letting her opinion and ways slip into the work assignments that she has taken from the leader. As in my example or doing follow up on voice messages, she may begin doing her follow up as she would do it herself not as the leader would do so. Jezebel would begin being the leader and influencing the organization through this task and basically be signing the leaders name to her actions. Her returned voice messages would be something like this, "The boss asked me, to give you call on his behalf about…." when if fact Jezebel may be speaking for her view of policy and not the leaders. She may totally ignore calls or squash the importance of calls that did not support her view and keep them from the leader. Jezebel at this point has successfully become a middleman of great influence, able to touch and influence many aspects of an organization with out being the leader.

Called into Question

When others question the influence of Jezebel, she is defended by the leader. The leader is so grateful for the work load that she has taken of his life he covers for her or looks the other way when questionable things come to his attention. Jezebel will take on so much responsibility that you will think the organization will collapse if you did take action against her. All this is a façade and self proclamation of her greatness and how difficult her job is to do. Jezebel is constantly sighing and making known to all how difficult her job is and how important it is as well. Jezebel also at this time reminds the leader of how she has selflessly helped him and does he want this to end, thus retaining her position in most cases.

Calling Yourself Into Question

One of the questions we must ask ourselves is what is the motivation to our actions? As I have mentioned there is nothing wrong with being an employee or part of an organization and giving of yourself to help others. Where it becomes an ethical issue is when your motive is to get power and advancement through dishonest means and at the expense of others. For any organization to be successful you need the best and most qualified people in all positions. So in order to be recognized we must have obvious good work ethics as well as skills for the position. We can call ourselves into question when we speak for our good works more than the good works speak for themselves. Jezebel is telling everyone how great she is when the humble and honest person's work usually speaks for its self.

We can also question ourselves when we are wanting specific compensation or favor for every thing extra we do. A common comment is "not my job." Many things are not our job but as we serve selflessly looking for promotion in the future those things will be your job and responsibility in the future, why not begin working on them now and become a help now? If you are part of an organization that has wise and fair leadership your good service will be recognized and honored in the future. You have to have wisdom to understand if you are at the right organization or not and trust that your day of promotion is coming someday. Manipulating and self promotion that Jezebel will do will turn off responsible leaders and seduce Ahab type leaders. Check your motives!

Chapter Sixteen

Changing Roles

If you have identified yourself as one of these characters, whether a good one or bad, that does not exempt one from shifting to one of the other roles. The best role to be is being a Jehu to fix things and then moving to a "kinder gentler" leader once things are brought into order.

I am a Jezebel

Not a pretty confession but an ethical one! If you can see how you have not had the right heart in serving and even have been manipulative with you actions, its great that you recognized it, now stop it! You may have harmed too many relationships and developed too many bad relationships also to continue to be a valid member of an organization, it may be time to move on and have a fresh start. Sadly of the characters mentioned in story more likely than not Jezebel is more likely to become an Ahab more than any other character. After to obtaining all power Jezebel will be subject to Jezebels serving under her as well. Remember too, that the best Jezebel is a seasoned veteran of manipulation and deceit.

Manipulation and deceit have become a life style not easy to break from, it has become a way of life.

Ahab is My Name

If you review your self and find, yes I have some Ahab tendencies, you can change. First you are a leader and you need to do your job and not let your self be manipulated by Jezebels. Not likely but an Ahab needs to become a Jehu for a season and right his wrongs and put them behind him. Just like Jezebel, Ahab may have allowed too many things to grow in a wrong way and may need a fresh start as well.

Once a Prophet Always A Prophet

If you have been the whistler blower like Elijah it will be hard to change your position. You will not be anyone's favorite person. You have made people at your level unsure about you at the best and angry at the worst and you have brought harm and trouble to leadership. The bad memories of bringing an organization to reality in most cases closes all doors to a peaceful future unless all leadership is completely changed. If you were an Elijah of a young age, this could be chalked up as experience, and then you could develop into what ever role life has for you in the future.

Jehu – Seasoned in War

If you think you are a Jehu, you are a seasoned veteran in taking command in situations and being successful in transforming an organization. You have already been many things, maybe an Elijah or even a Jezebel, but you have grown! Jehu sees and identifies the problems and takes care of the problems with out blinking an eye, so to speak.

Obadiah – A person of Peace

Obadiah seems like the person to be, hanging in while things get worse, hoping they get better soon, and not becoming enemies to either Jezebel or Elijah. The most likely change for Obadiah could be that he was once a vocal Elijah and has settled done to a quieter role. Obadiah could strengthen his position and become a Jehu as well. Being an Obadiah and hiding your real identity for an extended period of time may force one to take sides, either make a stand for what you believe or compromise your standards.

Chapter Seventeen
What to do?

How does one complete a book about such a common pattern of behavior that literally destroys organizations on a daily basis? The only way to complete this book is give a charge to be ethical in our lives both personally and in our dealings with organizations that we are members of or those we work with. Short cuts to success in life almost always are longer and usually incorporate taking on unprofessional and unethical practices for gain. These short cuts often have short term benefit and in most cases the fall out from the bad practice exposure, that will happen in time, sends you much further back I life. Think about the stories or personal experience when we pay to join a scheme to make money quickly and easily with some multilevel market plan or fancy product and in most cases you waste hours of time, offend all your friends and family, and lose that initial start up cash. Unethical practices of dishonesty and manipulation usually have a similar end or creates an atmosphere that most people are very uncomfortable with and good people will not want to be a part of that organization.

Character is contagious and America is and has been a great example great character throughout history. Here in America where the president is the most powerful position in the world, one person can step out of that position and another one into the position in a day without a shot being fired, without curfews, without a police state being put into effect, and without media blackouts. In other countries, also considered advanced, assassinations are common in every election as well as many other government actions are needed to squelch violence and uprisings. Why the difference? America has a history of great roots, great values, and great character. Many of the values that founded this country have been and are being chipped away but many of the standards of being honest and equitable in our relations are accepted by all though not practiced by all. If you are a leader, you should be practicing and touting honest and ethical behavior, rewarding and promoting those of with exemplary behavior in honesty and integrity.

With so much dirty campaigning in the election system and other scandals that surface in politics and Hollywood, one may think that we are a very corrupt society. The truth is that in some cultures many of these things are not scandals, they are accepted as part of the culture. We still have outrage about poor and unethical behavior though the outrage is weakened in some areas. The famous quote of Edmund Burke tells us what must not happen, "All that is necessary for the triumph of evil is that good men do nothing." Good men and women must do something and stand for what is right where we have a voice and influence.

One Organization At A Time
All it takes is for one organization to get it together and their great example will influence other organizations and individuals and make their organization become attractive and a model to others. Often we want to change the world starting at the top but serious effect can begin in one small organization. To be successful as an organization you must have a product or service that is needed by your community and no matter how ethical you are you won't succeed if you are promoting something that is dated or nor longer desired by people. If you have the product or service that is needed and it is coupled with honest and ethical behavior, you will have a going concern that will naturally draw people. Other organizations will know that they must change because they are

losing people to the more ethical environment. We can not succumbed to the thinking that, "What I do as an individual does not matter." What we all do does matter and many more people than we think are watching us and our behavior is influencing them as well.